for Leading Your Congregation

ADVOCATES FOR INCLUSIVENESS

Building a church that values and empowers all persons for full participation in the church and community

By the General Commission on the Status and Role of Women and the General Commission on Religion and Race

ADVOCATES FOR INCLUSIVENESS

Copyright © 2004 by Cokesbury

All rights reserved.
United Methodist churches and other official United Methodist bodies may reproduce up to 500 words from this publication, provided the following notice appears with the excerpted material: From *Advocates for Inclusiveness: 2005–2008*. Copyright © 2004 by Cokesbury. Used by permission.

Requests for quotations exceeding 500 words should be addressed to Permissions Office, Abingdon Press, P.O. Box 801, 201 Eighth Avenue South, Nashville, TN 37202-0801 or permissions@abingdonpress.com.

This book is printed on acid-free paper.

ISBN 0-687-00040-8

All Scripture quotations unless noted otherwise are taken from the *New Revised Standard Version of the Bible,* copyright 1989, by the Division of Christian Education of the National Council of the Churches of Christ in the United States of America. Used by permission. All rights reserved.

CONTENTS

Our Identity, Call, and Mission **4**

What Is My Job? **6**

Biblical and Theological Foundations for Inclusiveness **6**

What Are My Basic Responsibilities? **10**
    What Does the Coordinator Do?
    Quick-Start Tips

How Do I Relate to Other Groups in My Church? **12**

How Is the Ministry Group Organized? **13**

Models for Racial and Ethnic Inclusivness **14**

Checklist for an Inclusive Church **19**

Program Ideas on Behalf of All Women **23**
    Major Areas of Emphasis
    Sample Options for Action

Help! **28**

Resources **29**

General Agency Contacts .... Inside Back Cover

Our Identity, Call, and Mission

You are so important to the life of the Christian church! You have consented to be among a great and long line of people who have shared the faith and led others in the work of Jesus Christ. We have the church only because over the millennia people like you have caught the vision of God's kingdom and have claimed a place in the faith community to extend God's love to others. You have been called and have committed your unique passions, gifts, and abilities in a position of leadership, and this guide will help you understand some of the elements of that ministry and how it fits within the mission of your church and of The United Methodist Church.

"The mission of the Church is to make disciples of Jesus Christ. Local churches provide the most significant arena through which disciple-making occurs" (*The Book of Discipline of The United Methodist Church, 2004,* ¶120). The church is not only local but also global, and it is for everyone. Our church has an organizational structure through which we work, but it is a living organism as well. Each person is called to ministry by virtue of his or her baptism, and that ministry takes place in all aspects of daily life, not just within the walls of the church. Our *Book of Discipline* describes our mission to proclaim the gospel and to welcome people into the body of Christ, to lead people to a commitment to God through Jesus Christ, to nurture them in Christian living by various means of grace, and to send them into the world as agents of Jesus Christ (¶121). Thus, through you—and many other Christians—this very relational mission continues. (The *Discipline* explains the ministry of all Christians and the essence of servant ministry and leadership in ¶¶125–137.)

Essential Leadership Functions

Five functions of leadership are essential to strengthen and support the ministry of the church: identifying and supporting leaders as spiritual leaders, discovering current reality, naming shared vision, developing action plans, and monitoring the journey. This Guideline will help you identify these elements and set a course for ministry.

Lead in the Spirit

Each leader is a spiritual leader and has the opportunity to model spiritual maturity and discipline. John Wesley referred to the disciplines that cultivate a relationship with God as the "means of grace" and suggested several means: prayer, Bible study, fasting, public and private worship, Christian conversation, and acts of mercy. Local church leaders are strongly encouraged to identify their own spiritual practices, cultivate new ones as they grow in their own faith, and model and encourage these practices among their ministry team participants.

Discover Current Reality

"The way things are" is your current reality. How you organize, who does what, how bills get paid and plans get made are all building blocks of your current reality. Spend time with people who have been in this ministry and with your committee members to assess their view of how things are. Use "Christian conversation," one of the means of grace, not only to talk to others openly about their understanding of current reality but also to listen for the voice of God regarding your area of ministry.

Name Shared Vision

"The way things are" is only a prelude to "the way you want things to be." When the church is truly of God, it is the way God would envision it to be. Spend time with your committee and with other leaders in the church to discern the best and most faithful future you can imagine. How can you together identify your role and place in a faithful community that extends itself in its fourfold mission of reaching out and receiving people in the name of God, relating people to God, nurturing them in Christ and Christian living, and sending them forth as ministers into the world? Examine your committee's role and its place in that big picture and try to see yourselves as God's agents of grace and love.

Develop Action Plans

How do you get from here (your current reality) to there (your shared vision)? As a leader, one of your tasks is to hold in view both what is and what is hoped for so that you can build bridges to the future. These bridges are the interim goals and the action plans needed to accomplish the goals that will make your vision a reality. Remember that God may open up many (or different) avenues to that future, so be flexible and open to setting new goals and accepting new challenges. Action plans that describe how to meet interim goals should be specific, measurable, and attainable. While it is faithful to allow for the wondrous work of God in setting out bold plans, balance that boldness with realism. You and your committee will find information and tips here on developing and implementing the shared vision, the goals toward that vision, and the specific action plans that will accomplish the goals.

Monitor the Journey

A fifth responsibility of leaders is to keep an eye on how things are going. Setbacks will surely occur, but effective leaders keep moving toward their envisioned future. Not only will you monitor the progress of your committee's action plans to a faithful future but you will also be called to evaluate them in light of the ministry of the rest of the church. Immerse yourself and your plans in God's love and care. Voices from the congregation (both pro and con) may be the nudging of God to shift direction, rethink or plan, or move ahead boldly and without fear. Faithful leaders are attentive to the discernment of the congregation and to the heart of God in fulfilling the mission of the church.

What Is My Job?

Your task as coordinator of the ministry group is to help every ministry group, every committee, and every aspect of your church to be intentional about the full and equal participation of women and racial and ethnic persons in its life. As you advocate for an inclusive church, you are helping the church to reflect the fullness of the ministry of Christ.

> **Use of the Phrase W*omen and Racial and Ethnic Persons***
> One of the challenges in addressing issues related to full and equal participation of *women and racial and ethnic persons* is the language we use. We recognize that racial and ethnic women face discrimination both as women and as racial and ethnic persons. In this booklet we use the phrase *women and racial and ethnic persons* to communicate about issues of *all women* and of *all racial and ethnic persons*.

Biblical and Theological Foundations for Inclusiveness

Scripture tells us that in the beginning all people were created in God's image, thus becoming God's children, the household of God (Genesis 1:26-31). Throughout the biblical witness, we encounter God's call to humanity to live in right relationship with God and one another. The Commandments provide guidance to God's people about honoring God and the sacredness and dignity of God's creation. In Jesus Christ are the example and inspiration—who he is, what he taught, those whom he touched, healed, and called friends—of living fully and faithfully in God's image.

From the perspective of our faith, racism and sexism are sins that deny the wisdom of God's creation.

Racism Defined
Racism is a combination of the power by one race to dominate over another race and a value system based on an assumption that the dominant race is innately superior. In short, racial prejudice plus power equal racism. Personal racism is manifested through the individual expressions, attitudes, and behaviors that accept the assumptions of a racist value system. Institutional racism includes established social patterns that support implicitly or explicitly a racist value system.

Sexism Defined

Sexism is a system of beliefs or worldviews that regard women as inferior and men as superior. As with racism, any attitude, action, or structure that excludes women from full participation in power and responsibility (economic, social, or political) or declares them inferior because of their gender constitutes sexism. Sexism is a social and spiritual illness manifested in assimilation, socialization, harassment, discrimination, and oppression.

In Matthew 5:21-26, Jesus himself speaks out in a situation where people are insulted, ridiculed, and being called "fool" by others who believe themselves superior. For Jesus, these situations are not less than murder in the heart. Jesus is saying that the people of old were commanded not to kill (Exodus 20:13). But a person who is angry and insults and ridicules certain people has not learned the Bible's lesson of the sacredness and dignity of human beings. This kind of person must be judged in God's court, not in human courts.

Jesus takes such humiliating treatment by one human being toward another human being very seriously because it is dehumanizing—a denial of the person who is created in the image of God. It is a transgression showing a deliberate act of defiance against God. Jesus' words at the end of this Scripture passage say to us that acts of worship are not acceptable without first acting to be reconciled with our sisters and brothers. Because racism and sexism are social and spiritual illnesses, we are called to reflect on our experience and tradition in light of these and other biblical teachings.

Traditionally, United Methodists recognize fresh theological inquiry that arises from human experience of the reign of God. "Of crucial importance are concerns generated by great human struggles for dignity, liberation, and fulfillment—aspirations that are inherent elements in God's design for creation. These concerns are borne by theologies that express the heart cries of the downtrodden and the aroused indignation of the compassionate" (*Book of Discipline* ¶104).

Feminist, womanist, mujerista, and liberation theologies are examples of authentic Christian responses to the healing and redeeming Spirit of God. Inherent in feminist, womanist, and mujerista theologies is the affirmation of the full humanity of women. This affirmation of women contrasts with classic Western theology, which historically has defined humanity as male. Accordingly, authentic humanity includes a community of women, girls, boys, and men created in the likeness of God and rejects any claims of exclusively male norms or superiority by white Westerners and economically privileged classes, among others.

Theologies That Affirm All Humans

Feminist theologies include the study of the nature of God and human relation to God that draws on women's experience as a basic source of content and criterion of truth.

Womanist is from the black folk expression of mothers to female children, "You acting womanish," i.e. like a woman. Being grown, responsible, in charge, appreciating women's culture, women's strength and emotional flexibility and committed to the survival and wholeness of entire people, male and female, are characteristics of a womanist.
—Alice Walker

Mujerista theologies include Hispanic women's theologies which emerge from *mestizaje,* the convergence of very different cultures and histories (Amerindian, African, and Spanish) and liberation theologies. It is a communal theology drawing from the personal and lived experiences of Hispanic women.
—Ada María Isasi-Díaz

Liberation theologies are forged in a variety of contexts and are open to the gift of the kingdom (reign) of God—in protests against trampled human dignity, in struggles against the plunder of the vast majority of humankind, in liberating love, and in the building of a new, just, and comradely society.
—Gustavo Gutiérrez

Liberation theologies are sometimes described as "theologies from the underside of history," including the principle of "an option for the poor." According to Mumia Abu-Jamal, "It must come from the poor—a rebellion of the spirit that reaffirms their intrinsic worth based upon who they are rather than what they possess."

Your ministry in the area of inclusiveness is challenging and critical to the spiritual health of the church. Struggling to eliminate racism and sexism brings the church closer to becoming "one in Christ Jesus." Thus, building an inclusive church opens the door for people from different backgrounds to grow together in Christian community.

All persons are created in the likeness of God. Consequently, all people—regardless of color, language, nationality, class, education, gender, or lifestyle—are children of God. We are God's family, a family that is diverse because diversity is part of creation and a gift from God.

We cannot find any better expression of the church than the one described by Paul, using a human body as a model. He says of the church, "For just as the body is one and has many members, and all the members of the body, though many, are one body, so it is with Christ. For in the one Spirit we were all baptized into one body . . . and we were all made to drink of one Spirit" (1 Corinthians 12:12-13).

As Paul indicates, every member of the body is vitally important for the total church: "If one member suffers, all suffer together with it; if one member is honored, all rejoice together with it" (1 Corinthians 12:26).

When one member is discriminated against because he or she is different, the whole church suffers. When each member is treated as a person of sacred worth, the whole church rejoices and grows.

With the apostle Paul, the people of God join in creating and living in a world where the gifts of all persons, women and men, persons of all colors, hues, ethnic and national backgrounds, are celebrated, valued, and empowered for ministry, where "there is no longer Jew or Greek, . . . slave or free, . . . male and female; for all of you are one in Christ Jesus" (Galatians 3:28). You are elected to this glorious ministry.

What Are My Basic Responsibilities?

The goal of a ministry of inclusiveness is to examine how clearly the church's life reflects the full and equal participation of women and racial ethnic persons and to help the church strengthen its weaknesses in these areas.

The main functions of the ministry are:
- to keep the church council and the congregation aware of the meaning of the church's commitment to racial, ethnic, and gender inclusiveness in The United Methodist Church
- to recommend to the church council program opportunities for worship, fellowship, witness, study, nurture, and service with persons, groups, and congregations across racial, ethnic, and gender lines
- to consult with the pastor to keep the congregation and church council abreast of community issues and concerns affecting women and racial and ethnic persons and to make appropriate recommendations for outreach and advocacy
- to coordinate efforts to help your congregation experience and model the inclusive community of God.

As United Methodists, "we recognize that God made all creation and saw that it was good. As a diverse people of God who bring special gifts and evidences of God's grace to the unity of the Church and society, we are called to be faithful to the example of Jesus' ministry to all persons" (the *Book of Discipline* ¶138). This is our definition of inclusiveness.

What Does the Coordinator Do?

As coordinator of the ministry group, you will:
- lead the ministry group by scheduling meetings, facilitating the planning process, and communicating its plans and work to the church council and the congregation
- attend all meetings of the church council and participate fully in the planning process for all church programs
- work closely with other areas of ministry to recommend to them and to the church council specific program opportunities that will enhance the inclusiveness of the total church and its impact in the community
- learn about racism, sexism, discrimination, and prejudice so that you can understand their impact individually, culturally, and institutionally
- make inclusiveness everyone's agenda; serve as a catalyst to other ministry areas to integrate the concerns of women and racial and ethnic persons into all areas of your congregation.

Quick-Start Tips

Here are ten suggestions for getting started:

- Study this booklet so that you are informed about your responsibilities and about the theological and historical perspectives regarding women's status and roles, racial and ethnic diversity, and inclusiveness in The United Methodist Church.
- Talk with your pastor, the chairperson of the church council, and the previous chairperson of the inclusiveness ministry to learn how your ministry group fits into the church structure. Establish collaborative relationships and working styles.
- Convene a meeting of others who are or might become interested in working for the empowerment of women and for inclusiveness of all racial and ethnic persons. Begin by sharing your personal experiences and faith journeys. Invite dialogue on what people really think and feel. Remember that what you hear in church mirrors attitudes held in your community.
- Begin to collect the basic resources suggested on pages 29-30, or know where they are available.
- Start a notebook and files to collect information about racial and ethnic groups, diverse cultures, and women's issues locally and nationally.
- Contact your conference office or district superintendent to get the names of the coordinators in your district who advocate for inclusiveness. (Remember the terms for these groups may vary: Religion and Race, Status and Role of Women, etc.) Contact them to have your name placed on their mailing lists. Seek information about training and resources.
- Contact the General Commission on Religion and Race and the General Commission on the Status and Role of Women for resources and additional assistance as needed. (See page 28, "Help!" for ways to contact both commissions.)
- Be in touch with the network of both church-related and community organizations for support and information on racial and ethnic and women's issues.
- Work with your ministry group to set goals and activities for the year. Set related goals for yourself as coordinator so that you may become well informed about the contributions and concerns of racial and ethnic groups and women.
- Embark prayerfully. Remember that these issues touch deeply the very core of people's identities, social roles, and self-understandings—ideas and concepts formed over the course of years. Pray to God for guidance and wisdom to carry on your responsibilities. Pray for a change in attitudes and behavior for persons who have raised barriers between themselves and people of other races, ethnicities, cultural backgrounds, and gender.

How Do I Relate to Other Groups in My Church?

The coordinator of the ministry group is elected by the charge conference for a term of one year. According to paragraph 247.1 of the *Book of Discipline,* the charge conference shall be the connecting link between the local church and the general church and shall have general oversight of the church council. The church council shall provide for the planning and implementation of programs of nurture, outreach, witness, and resources in the local church and for the administration of its organization and temporal life. As coordinator of this ministry group, you are a member of the church council (or other appropriate body) with other church leaders to address the needs and opportunities of this ministry group.

You are encouraged to work with leaders of all program areas of the local church, giving particular attention to church and society for racial and ethnic concerns and to United Methodist Women and United Methodist Men for gender concerns. You are also encouraged to cooperate with the ministry group on church and society in its efforts to eliminate racism in our society and in the world.

Local units of United Methodist Women are outreach organizations, united through the Women's Division of the General Board of Global Ministries. Their primary focus is looking outward to the world, including ministries with women and children throughout the world. The local church ministry group or coordinator on Status and Role of Women provides a necessary focus inward to assist the congregation with the full and equal responsibility and participation of women in all aspects of the church's life.

You should also confer with the local church staff/pastor-parish relations committee to monitor hiring processes and employee support to ensure freedom from racial and gender bias.

How Is the Ministry Group Organized?

Because the local church has been given the freedom to organize as best fits its needs, you have several options for organizing your work:

- An individual may be elected as coordinator of a ministry group to work with the church council to plan inclusive church programs and ministries.
- In accordance with paragraph 254 of the *Book of Discipline*, the charge conference may elect annually a coordinator or ministry group chairperson for any or all of these areas: Christian unity and interreligious concerns, church and society, community volunteers, education, evangelism, higher education and campus ministry, missions, prayer advocacy, religion and race, status and role of women, stewardship, and worship.
- Where desirable, the charge conference may combine coordinators' or ministry group chairpersons' assignments.
- An individual may be elected as chairperson of outreach to help the congregation in concerns related to religion and race, status and role of women, Christian unity and interreligious concerns, church and society, and missions.

Organizational Options

According to the *Book of Discipline*, local churches may organize themselves in a manner that best fits their needs. As a result, your local church may address the concerns of women and racial ethnic persons in a variety of ways.

In this guide we use the term *coordinator* of ministry group to refer to the person or persons who carry out the leadership role(s) of advocating for an inclusive church. Two areas of particular emphasis on inclusiveness are religion and race and the status and role of women.

These two areas correspond to the areas of the general church that are charged with working toward the full and equal responsibility of racial and ethnic persons and women in the total life of The United Methodist Church: General Commission on Religion and Race (GCORR) and General Commission on the Status and Role of Women (GCSRW). Annual conferences and districts may also have groups or coordinators who address issues of inclusiveness and use such names as Annual Conference Commission on the Status and Role of Women (COSROW) and Annual Conference Commission on Religion and Race (CORR).

No matter how your local church organizes itself, your goal is to bring about the full and equal participation of women and racial ethnic persons in the life of the congregation.

Models for Racial and Ethnic Inclusiveness

The foundation for The United Methodist Church's commitment to racial inclusiveness and the elimination of racism is our relationship with God through Jesus Christ. Population growth projections for the twenty-first century point to an increasingly diverse society. The rapid growth of a racial and ethnic population in the United States, in particular, continues to be a challenge to the denomination's commitment to an inclusive church.

As your congregation works to bring about inclusiveness for racial ethnic persons, here are some examples of ways to embark on this journey. Keep in mind that these suggestions represent only a few of the many ways that you may proceed. See page 28, "Help!" for ways to contact the General Commission on Religion and Race for further information.

Diversity in Worship and Celebrations
Purpose: To raise the awareness of the different racial and ethnic backgrounds in The United Methodist Church through music, prayers, Scripture, sermon, and church calendar celebrations.

Some ways to do this are to:
- use a hymn or song each month from another racial ethnic tradition
- encourage the pastor to use inclusive language in the printed bulletin and to use bulletins that reflect inclusiveness.

Inclusive Language Is ...
Language for humanity that does not exclude anyone. This means language that is not ageist, sexist, racist, classist, or offensive to those with disabilities, and language about God that reflects the breadth of images for God in the biblical witness and experiences of people of God.

In its fullness, inclusive language is welcoming and draws from a variety of cultures, histories, languages, and manners of expression. With regard to gender, language in reference to humanity or God does not assume the male is generic. For example, *man* does not include *woman*; however, *humanity* does. *Mankind* does not include *women*; however, *humankind* does. *His* used generically does not include *her*; however, *their, his or her* does.

Other ways increase awareness are to:
- enable the congregation to learn prayers in other languages
- encourage the pastor to exchange pulpits with a pastor or layperson from another racial ethnic background.

- develop plans to maintain a mutual relationship with a congregation of a different racial ethnic background. Find ways to truly partner in ministry that move beyond superficial exchanges to ongoing cooperation and engagement of the two congregations.
- provide opportunities to experience different worship styles within the local community and to view videos or broadcasts of different worship styles to augment experiences.
- make plans to observe and celebrate ethnic heritages, such as Black History Month (February), Asian Pacific American Heritage Month (May), Native American Awareness Sunday (May), and Hispanic Heritage Month (mid-September to mid-October).

Transitional Congregations and Communities

Purpose: To increase the congregation's awareness to respond to the changes that are occurring in its surrounding community.

Here are some suggested procedures:
- Encourage the church council, through the appropriate ministry group, to identify the variety of racial and ethnic and cultural groups in the existing community.
- Once the group or groups have been identified, appoint a task group to secure cultural information. Identify community needs with the assistance of diverse community members.
- Review current ministries of the church to determine whether they address the identified needs, and adjust the ministries as necessary.
- Encourage the leadership to identify one or more congregations or community groups of a different racial and ethnic makeup with whom a learning and working relationship can be created.
- Encourage financial support for projects that will benefit the community in which the church is located and seeks to serve.
- Encourage the congregation to address societal and justice issues that affect the church's community.
- Provide a semiannual fellowship event for the church's community to help the congregation build ongoing relationships.

Racial and Ethnic Inclusiveness Mission and Ministry

Purpose: To enable the members to examine personal racial and cultural prejudice; to be more aware of and sensitive to racial, ethnic, and cultural diversity; to assist in strengthening relationships across racial lines; and to support the congregation in witnessing to the community.

Members might:
- Schedule a series of Bible studies in four- to six-week sessions to explore the biblical foundation of inclusiveness and diversity as a gift from God. Include points on the nature of racism.

- Provide opportunities for learning more about racial and cultural inclusiveness through reading and discussing books, listening to music, attending workshops and seminars, disseminating articles, and visiting museums. Make an effort to identify and include persons with expertise on topics of inclusiveness.
- Identify and train a small group of persons who have expressed a sensitivity to their participation in racism and who are willing to commit themselves for an extended period for time to meet as a support and study group.

Prejudice, Bigotry, and Discrimination Defined

There is a tendency to use words such as *prejudice, bigotry,* and *discrimination* interchangeably with *racism*. However, prejudice is an unfavorable opinion or feeling without knowledge, thought, or reason. Bigotry, on the other hand, is an extreme intolerance of any creed, belief, group, or opinion that differs from one's own. It is an acute form of prejudice. Discrimination takes action. It is the practices and policies exhibited based on prejudice or partiality. It is the power of making fine distinctions to express differential treatment.

Within this framework, all persons can discriminate on the basis of their prejudice such as gender, race, class, culture, or ethnicity. Prejudices are taught in our homes, schools, and churches. The media also contribute significantly to our opinions. The element of power distinguishes racism from prejudice, bigotry, and discrimination. Thus, we witness racism when the power of one group in society can enforce its prejudices against other groups.

- Identify a church with a different racial ethnic background from your own that is willing to cooperate in a series of family interchanges. Invite at least three families to participate in the worship service, church activities, and other special events. This process would be the beginning of building relationships, establishing new and lasting friendships, and developing greater insights, respect, genuine appreciation, and recognition.
- Plan a study using the resource "Step Toward Wholeness: Learning and Repentance." Offer a service of repentance and forgiveness for the sin of racism during Sunday worship. (For resources, contact General Commission on Christian Unity and Interreligious Concerns; telephone: 212-749-3553; fax: 212-749-3556.)
- Secure a facilitator who can assist Caucasian persons to be self-reflective by evaluating terms or phrases that may be perceived by others as stereotyped, degrading, or hurtful and by examining their attitudes and behaviors.

A Stereotype Is . . .
a negative or positive oversimplified and standardized conception or image of a person or group.

- Seek ways to learn more about the history and cultures of persons from a different racial or ethnic background who live inside or outside the community.
- Invite a friend or coworker of another racial or ethnic background to attend worship or another activity.
- Challenge manifestations of racism in the printed and spoken media.
- Educate the congregation on the definition of racial harassment. Provide support for persons experiencing racial harassment, and advocate for change.

Racial Harassment Is . . .
overt or covert abuse of persons based on race or ethnicity. This abuse can be manifested in ways such as language, inappropriate behavior, or other intimidating or unwanted action (see "Racial Harassment," *Book of Resolutions*).

Helping Youth Experience the Inclusive Community of God
Purpose: In cooperation with other ministry groups for youth and children, provide opportunities through which the youth will appreciate diversity and will experience inclusiveness.

- Identify youth who have been active participants in inclusiveness activities at church, at school, and in the community. From this group, organize a series of youth meetings with other youth in the church and community around the issue of racial ethnic relationships.
- Facilitate an ongoing relationship from the group of youth that have been meeting. Provide opportunities for attendance and participation at worship and other events.
- Sponsor social events such as bowling, basketball, picnics, or other activities that will ensure the participation and cooperation of youth from different racial and ethnic backgrounds.
- Engage in a historical dialogue and analysis with youth and their parents in a series of study and reflection to enable youth to understand the nature of racism and its implications for this century.
- Secure the assistance of the conference youth director to include opportunities for leadership and participation of racial and ethnic youth.
- Seek the help of the school in identifying common areas of concern and cooperation.
- Invite the pastor to promote active participation of the youth in all aspects of the church life.

Helping Children Experience the Inclusive Community of God

Purpose: To begin to develop an awareness of diversity and to share memories of the inclusive community through everyday experiences of young children and their families.

- Encourage the church council through the work area on children's ministry to establish a resource room for pictures, music, storybooks, and games that are multicultural and affirm diversity.
- Invite persons from different racial and ethnic backgrounds to visit during Sunday school, vacation Bible school, and worship so that children can be exposed to the diversity.
- Include pictures, stories, and language that are inclusive when working with children because the awareness of inclusiveness requires consistency and develops over long periods of time.
- Plan events that will promote diversity and encourage the children to respond to the various differences and similarities.
- Provide opportunities for the children to participate in worship with songs, dance, poetry, plays, and biblical stories that demonstrate God's gift of inclusiveness.
- Encourage diversity in the observance of a children's Sabbath.

Cross-Racial Appointments

Purpose: To cultivate a caring environment in which a responsive, compassionate, and viable multicultural, multiracial ministry may be developed through the appointment of a pastor from a different racial ethnic background.

- Design and provide leadership to ensure that the committee on staff/pastor-parish relations is supportive of the concept of open itinerancy and experience workshops on inclusiveness, racism, and cultural awareness as needed to enhance effectiveness as facilitators for congregational acceptance of the process.
- Ask the pastor to share biblical insights and theological reflections about inclusiveness through the church newsletter, sermons, meetings, Bible studies, and individual conferences.
- Encourage other ministry groups to provide ongoing opportunities for the congregation to engage in open, honest, and candid dialogue about their fears, concerns, and affirmations.
- Encourage the church council through appropriate work areas or committees to provide opportunities for the congregation to experience varied styles and forms of worship through pulpit and choir exchanges.
- Organize an intercessory prayer group that focuses specifically on the vision of racial inclusiveness of the congregation.
- In consultation with the committee on staff/pastor-parish relations, cultivate a group of people who will serve as a means of support for the pastor, spouse, and children for ongoing communication and sharing.
- Help the congregation understand cross-racial appointment as part of the connectional church and the denomination's commitment to inclusiveness.

Checklist for an Inclusive Church

As the ministry group(s) working to bring about the full and equal participation of women and racial and ethnic persons in the life of the church, you may use this checklist to begin examining behavior and attitudes toward women, racial and ethnic persons, disabled persons, and persons of all ages and economic classes. Your findings can point you toward areas in which to take action.

In assessing the inclusiveness of your church, please read the statements listed below. If the statement reflects your church, place a check mark next to it. If the statement does not reflect your church, this area may need attention. Your church is on the way to becoming an inclusive church if at least half of the statements in each section are checked.

Attitudes

_____ All persons are understood to be equal creations of God, made in God's image, and worthy of God's blessings.

_____ Experiences of all persons are included in all facets of the life of the church, such as sermon examples and special observances.

_____ Leaders in the congregation have had training on issues related to sexism, racism, and ageism other isms to encourage diverse ministries for all persons in the community.

_____ Ministry groups develop and encourage participation in programs to eliminate sexism, racism, and ethnocentrism of all forms as they may exist in the life of the congregation.

_____ When expert advice is needed, experts are sought from diverse backgrounds based on their education, talents, and experience rather than on stereotypical images. For example, are women and racial ethnic persons considered when seeking attorneys, contractors, architects, and other professionals?

Education

_____ Members of Sunday school or church school are provided the opportunity to use curriculum that reflects the diversity of society.

_____ The Christian education program offers educational opportunities related to the history, culture, and concerns of persons who reflect the diversity of society.

_____ Pictures, symbols, and artifacts representing the racial ethnic, cultural, and gender diversity of society are visible throughout our church.

_____ The United Methodist Church "Charter for Racial Justice" has been studied using the study guide prepared by the Women's Division of the General Board of Global Ministries.

_____ Staff and leaders of the congregation have studied the goals of Project Equality and have incorporated the goals when purchasing decisions are made for the church.

Worship

_____ All members have opportunities to serve in various aspects of the worship service: ushers, acolytes, lay liturgists, and other roles.

_____ Guest preachers are invited based on their abilities rather than on stereotypical images.

_____ The congregation has opportunities in worship to experience music, liturgy, and prayers that reflect diverse representations of culture and gender.

_____ When speaking of God and humanity, staff and leaders use a range of inclusive language and images that reflect images from the Bible, our traditions, and experience.

Leadership

_____ All members of the congregation with appropriate skills and interest receive opportunities to share their gifts in the church's ministries and committees as members and leaders.

_____ The church welcomes and embraces all pastors who are appointed to their congregation, regardless of their racial ethnicity, culture, and gender.

_____ All persons are welcomed and encouraged to work in positions that fit their gifts without limiting them to stereotypical roles.

_____ The church is intentional in offering training opportunities for all persons, regardless of race, ethnicity, or gender.

_____ The church responds to the needs of all its members by providing childcare, accessible facilities, and directional signs as evidence of its hospitality.

Fellowship

_____ The congregation has opportunities on a regular basis for fellowship with persons from varied backgrounds and experiences.

Witness, Mission, Church, and Society

_____ Church organizations advocate for the dignity and rights of all persons in the community.

_____ Ministry areas of the church integrate concerns of all groups of people and raise the awareness of these concerns so that all persons may participate fully in the life of the congregation.

_____ Outreach programs include projects that encourage members to form lasting relationships with diverse persons.

_____ The church demonstrates its hospitality and receptivity by providing accessible facilities, childcare for participants, and a spirit of openness and warmth to persons from diverse backgrounds.

_____ Bulletins, flyers, and newsletters show photos that represent a cross section of the community residents.

_____ Helping the church to become more inclusive becomes everyone's agenda rather than the agenda of only a few persons.

Personnel

_____ The committee on staff/pastor-parish relations has developed a process for assuring equal employment hiring practices in regard to women and racial ethnic persons.

_____ The committee on staff/pastor-parish relations collaborates with the pastor, spouse, and family to ensure that adequate support systems are identified and provided.

_____ The committee on staff/pastor-parish relations has developed sexual and racial harassment policies and provided training for all staff and the congregation.

_____ The committee on staff/pastor-parish relations has developed a local church policy on sexual misconduct and has educated the congregation on these matters.

_____ The congregation has initiated a study of the "Charter for Racial Justice" provided by the Women's Division of the General Board of Global Ministries.

Program Ideas on Behalf of All Women

Recognizing that every person, woman or man, is a full and equal part of God's human family, The United Methodist Church is committed to the full and equal responsibility and participation of women in the total life and mission of the church.

As your congregation works to bring about inclusiveness for women, here are some examples of ways to embark on this journey. Keep in mind that these suggestions represent only a few of the many ways that you may proceed. For further information, see page 28, "Help!" for ways to contact the General Commission on the Status and Role of Women.

Major Areas of Emphasis

Three key words have come to signify the major areas of work of this ministry group on behalf of women: *advocate, catalyst,* and *monitor*.

As **advocate**, speak on behalf of women, enabling them to claim their rightful place in decision-making arenas, to ensure that the church has the benefit of the wisdom, life experiences, and perspectives of women. Remember that to be an advocate is to stand with and share the pain and joy as women grow. Consider these opportunities for advocacy:

- Work with individual women who are employed by the church—both lay and clergy—and who have experienced discrimination on the basis of their gender.
- Work with women who, in carrying out designated leadership roles or in receiving services from the church, experience sex discrimination, unequal treatment, or inadequate support.
- Take the initiative to make changes on behalf of all women or special groups of women such as laywomen, racial and ethnic women, clergywomen, and single women.
- Advocate on behalf of an individual woman who is experiencing discrimination or harassment because of her gender.
- Provide support and healing for women as they experience significant changes in attitudes and behaviors.

As **catalyst**, seek to bring together previously isolated and seemingly incompatible elements. To be a catalyst is to endeavor to bring about new perceptions, new roles, and new empowerment for women in the church.

Steps in this catalyst process may include the following:
- Work simultaneously with the structures of the church and with women to ensure full and equal participation of women.
- Identify women and groups of women whose needs are not being adequately met by the church.
- Take an inventory of their needs and the expectations of the church.
- Determine where, within the church, the needs of these women would most appropriately be addressed—if the church were fully inclusive, aware, and responsive.
- Train women to take responsibility in their own arenas—to become catalysts on behalf of themselves and other women.

As **monitor**, examine the ongoing life and commitment of the church in areas related to inclusiveness. You may begin with the following:

- Monitor church publications, sermons, activities, and meetings for inclusive and gender-free language and imagery. (See p. 14 for a definition of inclusive language.)
- Monitor the numbers of women in leadership and the quality of their participation on committees. Are women involved in forming policy as well as in roles that carry out policies set by others?
- Formally or informally survey church members for their attitudes on women in leadership, inclusive language, and other issues relative to women.
- Report results and resurvey periodically (for example, once every two to four years) to measure changes and to provide ongoing reflection of your church's inclusiveness of women.

Sample Options for Action

The following ideas offer only a taste of options available for action that your ministry group may take on behalf of women. You may contact the General Commission on the Status and Role of Women for more ideas for local church ministry. (See page 28 for ways to contact the commission.)

Children and Youth
- Work with the youth age-level coordinator to plan programs for teenage girls that promote self-esteem, assertiveness, and self-confidence.
- With the children's and youth age-level coordinators, examine ways to involve girls and boys in church activities that honor their individual differences. Monitor for inappropriate divisions of activities by gender.
- Promote age-appropriate education about sexual and physical abuse for children and the examination of dating norms and related issues, such as date rape, for youth and young adults.

Consensus
- Provide training for church leaders in consensus style of decision making, and encourage its use as an appropriate decision-making method.
- Brainstorm with the church council about ways to increase participation in decision making. Consider meeting seating arrangement, training, roles of the pastor or other staff, and factors that might be intimidating or confusing to new members or less verbal members. Take steps to implement the best ideas.
- With an adult class or discussion group, reflect candidly on the way different groups make decisions: married couples, youth peer groups, church committees, family groups, society at large. What are advantages and disadvantages of each method?

Consensus is ...
Consensus is a method of decision making commonly used by groups that place high value on mutual trust and the valuing of persons. In this method, a workable decision represents a state of unanimity—a decision that every person can live with. In the decision-making process, each person's opinion is heard and valued. Emphasis is on the best possible corporate decision, not on who wins or loses

Groups
- Find out about the variety of women in your congregation. Mothers, daughters, and wives often are recognized but may need additional or different kinds of support. Encourage awareness of needs and interests for women of all ages and diverse life experiences. Sponsor events and groups specifically for those who often are overlooked in church life.
- Start new social groups that depart from traditional groupings such as young married couples or singles and instead combine a variety of ages and family forms.
- Consider an alternative to a mother-daughter event that allows women without children to be full participants. Consider honoring women who have had formative roles in the lives of those attending.
- Designate a bulletin board for announcements and information of interest to women, including information about supportive, social, or study groups specifically for women.
- Start a women's center in the church for groups of women to gather.

Heritage
Collect the stories of clergywomen who have served your congregation. In 2006 The United Methodist Church celebrates the fiftieth anniversary of the full ordination of women. Visit the Web site of the General Commission on Archives and History for guidelines on how to contribute stories.

- Make a presentation on women's issues to the confirmation class; share some history of women in The United Methodist Church with the class.
- Work with your church historian to produce the names and accomplishments of women leaders of the past; celebrate these contributions in exhibits displaying pictures, pamphlets, and memorabilia. Update the church history with the information you have gathered.
- Begin a record, to be kept in the church, of the activities of women; update it annually.
- Establish a Foremothers Sunday or encourage the use of Mother's Day to celebrate women in church history.
- Consider future generations by recording oral and written histories of the women who are at work in your church now or are in the memories of older members. Update older records to preserve the full names of these women (for example, Bessie Brown Jones in addition to Mrs. Joseph Jones).
- Participate in community observances or plan an observance at your own church of Women's History Month (March). (See also pp. 14-15 for ethnic celebrations.)

Listen
- Promote opportunities for women and men to talk together about women's issues and the implications for men. As one possibility, hold a not-for-women-only listening event with the United Methodist Men, asking how women's changing roles have affected their lives.
- Hold a women-only retreat and talk together about what hurts, what heals, what worries, and what comforts women. Use what you learn to evaluate the effectiveness of your church in meeting the needs of women; protect confidences.
- If women and men seem to approach a subject differently, try a fish bowl discussion, alternating women-only and men-only groups, while the others just listen. Then have the whole group share observations.

Nominations
- Recruit women to serve on committees and in leadership positions. Compile a list of those women, including their interests, experiences, and so forth. Submit the list to the nominating committee.
- Remember to nominate for the nominating committee men and women who share a commitment to inclusiveness in the church. (These people are nominated from the floor at the annual charge conference or church conference. Ask them in advance if they would be willing to serve.)
- Build self-esteem in others by encouraging wider use of their talents, recognizing services performed, and offering opportunities to gain new skills. Work to make your church a safe place for women to try new things.

Sexism

(See p. 7 for a definition of sexism.)

- Observe your congregation in its life and ministry. Are men and women treated differently? Is there discrimination according to gender? Bring attention to the situations in which women are treated unfairly or inequitably.
- Consider working with your local church coordinator of children's ministries to plan a special day or Sunday school session to explore roles of girls and boys in church and society.
- Find out what counseling and related resources are available for members of your congregation. Are women valued as full and equal creations of God?
- Work with your local church ministry area coordinator on Religion and Race to promote understanding in the congregation of the roots of oppression. Work together to discover ways to raise awareness of the double oppression faced by racial and ethnic women.

Violence

- Support local agencies: shelters for battered women, crisis centers, incest or rape survivors groups. Post flyers and telephone numbers prominently. Offer meeting space in your building.
- Remember the survivors of abuse in worship and worship planning. Work with your pastor and other church leaders to break the silence about abuse, harassment, and violence against women. Consider ways silence may be broken through sermons, prayers, or special services of healing, remembering always to have adequate support persons available for those who may seek help.
- Promote education for men and boys and for women and girls about violence against women and about the characteristics of abuse. Consider planning an event with your United Methodist Youth Fellowship about date rape, harassment, media, and values in relationships.

Sexual Abuse is . . .

ordinarily thought of as a sexual invasion of the body by force. Sexual abuse may be rape, sexual assault, indecent exposure, statutory rape, involuntary or voluntary deviant sexual intercourse with a child, promotion of prostitution, pornography of children, indecent assault, and aggravated indecent assault.

Sexual Harassment is . . .

any unwanted sexual advance or demand, either verbal or physical, that is reasonably perceived by the recipient as demeaning, intimidating, or coercive. Sexual harassment must be understood as an exploitation of a power relationship rather than as an exclusively sexual issue. Sexual harassment includes, but is not limited to, the creation of a hostile or abusive working environment resulting from discrimination based on gender.

Sexual Misconduct is...
when it occurs within a ministerial relationship a betrayal of sacred trust, a violation of the ministerial role, and the exploitation of those who are vulnerable in that relationship. It occurs when a person within a ministerial role of leadership (lay or clergy, pastor, educator, counselor, youth leader, or other position of leadership) engages in sexual contact or sexualized behavior with a congregant, client, employee, student, staff member, coworker, or volunteer within the ministerial relationship.

Help!

Remember as you carry out your ministry as advocate for inclusiveness that this Guideline is just that—a guide for your journey. We hope that this Guideline will encourage you on the journey of building a church that values and empowers all persons for full participation in the church and community. Your gifts for this ministry are vital to the church. Thank you for your faithful walk on this way of following Christ.

We encourage you to keep the following page in a convenient location because we want to hear from you. You may reach both commissions in a variety of ways. Your questions, your struggles, and your ideas are important to us.

General Commission on Religion and Race
100 Maryland Avenue, NE, Suite 400
Washington, D.C. 20002
Voice: 202-547-2271
Fax: 202-547-0358
E-mail: gcorr@erols.com.
Web site: www.umc.org/gcrr.

General Commission on the Status and Role of Women
1200 Davis Street
Evanston, IL 60201
Voice: 800-523-8390
847-869-7330
Fax: 847-869-1466
E-mail: gcsrw@gcfa.org.
Web site: www.umc.org/gcsrw

Project Equality
7132 Main Street
Kansas City, MO 64114-1406
Telephone: 877-734-7336 or 816-361-9222
Fax: 816-361-8997

Resources

This brief list of resources can help launch your leadership journey. You will find much more detailed lists of resources and program materials on our Internet Web sites, as indicated earlier. Call us to discuss particular needs.

- *The Book of Discipline of The United Methodist Church,* 2000. United Methodist Publishing House. Available from Cokesbury. This basic reference for our church's organization offers information on local church structures as well as annual conference and general church structures.

- *Antiracism Study/Action Guides:*
- *Confronting the Sin* by Elaine Jenkins
- *The Gift of Diversity* by Eric H. Law
- *Overcoming Racism's Economic Legacies* by J. Phillip Wogaman Produced jointly by the General Board of Church and Society and the General Commission on Religion and Race. Available from GCORR.

- *Building a New Community: God's Children Overcoming Racism.* Available through Cokesbury.

- *Diversity Is . . .* A video produced by the General Commission on Religion and Race, in cooperation with United Methodist Communications. Study guide included. Time: 15-1/2 minutes. Available through EcuFilm.

- *The Flyer,* quarterly newsletter of the General Commission on the Status and Role of Women (GCSRW), 1200 Davis Street, Evanston, IL 60201. Available by subscription directly from GCSRW.

- Guidelines for Leading Your Congregation, 2005–2008. Abingdon Press. A set of guidelines (this Guideline is one of the set) providing guidance for persons responsible for the administration and programs of the local church. Available from Cokesbury or Discipleship Resources.

- *Indicators of Institutional Racism, Sexism and Classism: Some Suggested Responses.* Available from the Office of Inclusiveness and Justice, National Council of Churches of Christ in the USA, 475 Riverside Drive, Room 820, New York, NY 10115.

- *Interpreter,* monthly program journal for local church leaders. Seven copies are provided free to each local church; additional subscriptions available at a nominal cost; ask your pastor or order from United Methodist Communications, 615-742-5400.

- *Language of Hospitality: Intercultural Relations in the Household of God* by Anne Streaty Wimberly and Edward Powell Wimberly. Available from Cokesbury.

- *The Monitor,* quarterly newsletter of the ministry of the General Commission on Religion and Race. Available at no charge from GCORR to anyone who asks to be added to the mailing list.

- *When the Church Speaks: A Guide to the Social Principles.* A booklet giving the social policies of The United Methodist Church as set forth by General Conference. Available from Cokesbury.

- *Telling Their Stories: The History of Women in the Local Church, A Resource Packet.* Prepared by the General Commission on Archives and History; telephone: 973-408-3189.

- *You Can't Do It Alone: Fighting Racism.* Video with study guide designed for young adults ages fifteen through twenty-five. Available from Evangelical Lutheran Church in America, ELCA Distribution Service, 426 South Fifth Street, P.O. Box 1209, Minneapolis, MN 55440; 800-328-4648.

There may have been some changes in *Discipline* paragraph numbers or wording after this Guideline was printed. We regret any inconvenience.